# TABLE OF CONTENT

# AUTHENTIC JAPANESE COOKBOOK

## Learn to Make Japanese Dishes for Beginners Classic and Modern Recipes Made Easy at Home

### By: Carlie Gerhard

# INTRODUCTION

Do you wish to experience unique Japanese flavors by preparing some delectable and authentic Japanese dishes at home? You've come to the correct location! This guidebook will introduce you to some of the most famous Japanese recipes and words you like. Whether they are from Southern or Northern Japan, the entire Island has its own culture and traditions. History has had a significant impact on Japanese culinary standards and cuisine. Also, geographical and climatic influences contribute to diverse tastes and shapes in Japanese food. So, today, you'll learn all about the richness and complexity of Asian cuisine.

Japanese Cookbook, in particular, will introduce you to Japanese cuisine and culinary culture in an entertaining style you have probably never tasted before. It compiles a wide range of Japanese recipes in one spot. This cookbook is ideal for anyone who enjoys cooking nutritious meals and trying new and unusual flavors. You may make a whole Japanese menu at home with the help of this Japanese cuisine cookbook, or you can prepare all of the distinctive Japanese recipes for special occasions and festivals.

This thorough cookbook contains familiar Japanese dishes and those you may not have heard of. You can discover everything from nourishing folded eggs for breakfast to all the comforting meat and noodles soups, Japanese desserts, drinks, entrees, and healthy Japanese salads. Furthermore, these recipes are written so that even those unfamiliar with Japanese culture, food, and language can attempt to cook them at home without trouble.

Japanese culinary culture and cuisine are pretty unique. Soy sauce, spices, vegetables, and meat are all used significantly. And, if you want to incorporate all those healthy nutrients into your diet, read this book thoroughly, and you'll find all your answers right now.

# ESSENTIAL INGREDIENTS OF JAPANESE CUISINE

**Rice:** Rice is a common ingredient in many Japanese meals, including sushi, sashimi, and donburi. For Japanese cuisine, it's crucial to utilize premium rice because it will significantly alter the flavor of your food.

**Soy sauce:** Using soybeans, salt, and wheat, soy sauce is a fermented sauce. To impart taste and saltiness, it is a common ingredient in Japanese cuisine. Choose a soy sauce that is appropriate for the food you are creating from the variety that is available.

**Mirin:** Used in Japanese cooking to enhance sweetness and umami, mirin is a sweet rice wine. Additionally, it is used to provide a glossy finish to food and deglaze cookware.

**Sake:** Japanese cuisine uses sake, a fermented rice wine, to enhance taste and complexity. It may be used to deglaze pans, prepare sauces, marinade meat and seafood, and more.

**Dashi:** Dashi is a stock produced from dried bonito flakes and seaweed called kombu. Numerous Japanese foods, such as miso soup, udon noodles, and soba noodles, are built upon it.

**Miso:** Used in Japanese cuisine to impart taste and saltiness, miso is a fermented soybean paste. Miso soup and other foods are also prepared with it.

**Wasabi:** The rhizome of the wasabia japonica plant is used to make a strong, green paste known as wasabi. For sushi and other Japanese meals, it is a condiment.

**Shichimi togarashi:** Shichimi togarashi is a time-honored Japanese spice blend that has been carefully curated using seven distinct spices to enhance the flavor profile and impart a pleasant level of spiciness to various culinary preparations. Typically, sesame seeds, nori (seaweed), poppy seeds, hemp seeds, sansho pepper, and ginger are used to make it.

# ESSENTIAL EQUIPMENT FOR JAPANESE COOKING

**Heavy-bottomed pot**: Because it is adaptable and can be used for a range of jobs, including simmering, grilling, and deep-frying, a heavy-bottomed pot is a must for Japanese cuisine.

**Rice cooker:** While not necessary, a rice cooker is a practical method to make consistently delicious rice.

**Sharpening stone:** A sharpening stone is necessary to maintain the edge on your blades. Japanese cookery calls for the use of sharp knives since they enable accurate cutting.

**Cutting board:** A decent cutting board is necessary in every kitchen, but Japanese cuisine places a premium on this item. Pick a cutting board that is big enough to fit the ingredients you'll be chopping, and make sure it's made of something sturdy like wood or bamboo.

**Chopsticks:** Eating Japanese food traditionally involves using chopsticks. They help you handle food precisely during cooking, which is another application for them.

# BASIC TECHNIQUES OF JAPANESE CUISINE

**Cutting:** In Japanese cookery, cutting is a crucial skill. In Japanese cooking, a number of various cutting methods, including slicing, dicing, and mincing, are employed. Learning the fundamentals of cutting can help you correctly prepare your ingredients.

**Simmering:** Japanese cuisine uses the gentle cooking technique of simmering to prepare meat, fish, and vegetables. To preserve their taste and nutrition, foods must be simmered at a low temperature.

**Grilling:** In Japanese cookery, grilling is a common technique. Meat, fish, and vegetables may all be cooked in it. To keep the food soft and juicy while grilling Japanese food, it's crucial to utilize high heat and cook the meal rapidly.

**Steaming:** Japanese cuisine uses the healthy cooking technique of steaming to prepare meat, fish, and vegetables. The flavor and nutrients of the food are preserved throughout the mild cooking process of steaming.

**Deep-frying:** A common technique in Japanese cookery is deep-frying. Meat, fish, and vegetables may all be cooked in it. To keep the food crispy and golden brown while deep-frying Japanese food, it's crucial to use premium oil and cook the meal at the proper temperature.

# SUSHI SENSATIONS

## CLASSIC NIGIRI SUSHI

### Ingredients:

- 1 cup sushi rice
- Two tablespoons of rice vinegar
- Fresh fish or seafood of your choice (such as tuna, salmon, shrimp, or eel)
- Soy sauce for dipping
- Wasabi and pickled ginger for serving

### Instructions:

1. Prepare the sushi rice per the directions on the package.

2. Combine cooked rice and rice vinegar in a small bowl.

3. Wet your hands and shape small portions of rice into oblong shapes.

4. Place a fresh fish or seafood slice on each rice mound.

5. Serve nigiri sushi with soy sauce, wasabi, and pickled ginger on the side.

6. Enjoy!

## SPICY TUNA ROLLS

### Ingredients:

- Sushi rice
- Nori (seaweed) sheets
- Canned tuna
- Sriracha sauce

- Mayonnaise
- Soy sauce

## Instructions:

1. Prepare the sushi rice per the directions on the package.

2. mix canned tuna with sriracha sauce and mayonnaise to taste in a bowl.

3. Lay a nori sheet on a bamboo mat or plastic wrap.

4. Cover the nori with a thin layer of sushi rice, leaving about 1 inch uncovered at the top.

5. Place a spicy tuna mixture line in the rice's center.

6. Roll tightly using the bamboo mat or plastic wrap, applying gentle pressure to shape the roll.

7. Slice into bite-sized pieces using a sharp knife.

8. Serve with soy sauce for dipping. Enjoy!

## DRAGON ROLL

## Ingredients:

- Nori seaweed sheets
- Sushi rice
- Fresh salmon
- Avocado
- Cucumber
- Soy sauce
- Wasabi paste

## Instructions:

1. Prepare sushi rice and let it cool.

2. Lay a sheet of nori on a bamboo sushi mat.

3. Spread a thin layer of sushi rice on the nori, leaving 1 inch at the top uncovered.

4. Place thin slices of fresh salmon, avocado, and cucumber in the center of the rice.

5. Roll tightly using the bamboo mat, applying gentle pressure.

6. Cut into bite-sized pieces using a sharp knife.

7. Serve with soy sauce and wasabi paste on the side. Enjoy!

## VEGETARIAN SUSHI

## Ingredients:

- Sushi rice
- Sheets of nori (seaweed)
- Assorted vegetables (carrots, cucumber, avocado)
- Soy sauce
- Wasabi
- Pickled ginger

## Instructions:

1. Prepare the sushi rice per the directions on the package, then set aside to cool.

2. Lay a sheet of nori on a bamboo sushi mat.

3. Leaving a tiny border at the top, cover the nori with a thin coating of sushi rice.

4. Place thinly sliced vegetables on top of the rice.

5. Roll the bamboo mat tightly from bottom to top, using gentle pressure to shape the sushi roll.

6. Slice the roll into bite-sized pieces using a sharp knife.

7. Serve with soy sauce, wasabi, and pickled ginger. Enjoy!

## SUSHI BOWL

### Ingredients:

- 2 cups sushi rice
- 1 cup cooked shrimp, chopped
- One avocado, sliced
- One cucumber, sliced
- One carrot, shredded
- One nori sheet, cut into thin strips
- Soy sauce for serving

### Instructions:

1. Prepare the sushi rice as directed on the package.

2. In a bowl, add a bed of sushi rice.

3. Top with chopped shrimp, avocado, cucumber, and shredded carrots.

4. Sprinkle nori strips on top.

5. Serve with soy sauce on the side. Enjoy!

# SASHIMI DELIGHTS

## Ingredients:

- Fresh sashimi-grade fish (tuna, salmon, or yellowtail)
- Soy sauce
- Wasabi
- Pickled ginger
- Sesame seeds

## Instructions:

1. Slice the fresh fish into thin pieces.

2. Arrange the slices on a plate.

3. Serve with soy sauce, wasabi, pickled ginger, and sesame seeds on the side.

4. Dip each slice in soy sauce and add a touch of wasabi before enjoying.

# TERIYAKI SALMON SUSHI

## Ingredients:

- Four salmon fillets
- 1/2 cup soy sauce
- 1/4 cup mirin (sweet rice wine)
- Two tablespoons brown sugar
- Two tablespoons honey
- One teaspoon of grated ginger
- One teaspoon of garlic paste
- Nori sheets (seaweed)
- Sushi rice

## Instructions:

1. Set the oven's temperature to 400°F or 200°C.

2. mix soy sauce, mirin, brown sugar, honey, ginger, and garlic paste in a small bowl.

3. Transfer the salmon fillets and the teriyaki marinade to a shallow plate.

4. Marinate for at least 30 minutes.

5. Meanwhile, cook sushi rice according to package instructions and let it cool.

6. Lightly oil and heat a nonstick skillet over medium-high heat.

7. Remove salmon from marinade and place skin-side down in the skillet.

8. Cook until well done, about 3 minutes on each side.

9. Please remove the heat source and rest for several minutes before slicing it into thin strips.

10. Place a nori sheet on a bamboo sushi mat and spread sushi rice evenly over it, leaving a small border at the top edge.

11. Arrange slices of teriyaki salmon across the center of the rice.

12. Roll tightly using the bamboo mat and wetting the top border to seal it.

13. Slice into bite-sized pieces using a sharp.

# CALIFORNIA ROLLS

## Ingredients:

- 1 cup sushi rice
- Eight nori sheets
- Two tablespoons of rice vinegar
- One avocado, thinly sliced
- 1/2 cucumber, julienned
- 1/2 pound imitation crab meat

## Instructions:

1. Prepare the sushi rice per the directions on the package, then set aside to cool.

2. Lay a sheet of nori on a bamboo sushi mat.

3. Spread a thin layer of rice onto the nori, leaving a small border at the top.

4. Place avocado, cucumber, and crab meat in the center of the rice.

5. Roll tightly using the bamboo mat, applying gentle pressure.

6. Wet the top border with water to seal the roll.

7. Slice into bite-sized pieces and serve with soy sauce and wasabi if desired. Enjoy!

# INARI SUSHI

## Ingredients:

- 1 cup sushi rice
- 4-6 Inari pockets

- Two tablespoons of soy sauce
- One tablespoon mirin
- One tablespoon sugar
- One tablespoon of rice vinegar

## Instructions:

1. Prepare the sushi rice per the directions on the package.

2. To make the spice combination, combine the soy sauce, mirin, sugar, and rice vinegar

in a small bowl.

3. Transfer sushi rice into a large bowl and gently mix in the seasoning mixture once it is cooked.

4. Allow the seasoned rice to cool slightly.

5. Gently open each inari pocket and stuff them with a spoonful of seasoned sushi rice.

6. Serve and enjoy your Inari Sushi!

## EEL AND AVOCADO ROLLS

## Ingredients:

- One eel fillet
- One ripe avocado
- Nori seaweed sheets
- Sushi rice
- Soy sauce

## Instructions:

1. Cook the eel fillet until it is tender and flaky.

2. Cut the avocado into thin slices.

3. Place a sheet of nori seaweed on a bamboo mat or clean surface.

4. Spread sushi rice evenly over the nori, leaving a small border at one end.

5. Lay the eel and avocado slices on top of the rice.

6. Roll tightly using the bamboo mat, starting from the end with the filling.

7. Slice into bite-sized pieces using a sharp knife.

8. Serve with soy sauce for dipping. Enjoy!

# RAMEN REVOLUTION
## SHOYU RAMEN

## Ingredients:

- Two packages of ramen noodles
- 4 cups of chicken or vegetable broth
- One tablespoon of soy sauce
- One tablespoon of mirin
- One teaspoon of sesame oil
- Sliced green onions for garnish
- Soft-boiled eggs for topping

## Instructions:

1. Prepare the ramen noodles per the directions on the package and set them aside.

2. bring the vegetable stock to a boil in a huge pot.

3. Add soy sauce, mirin, and sesame oil to the broth and stir well.

4. Divide the cooked ramen noodles into bowls.

5. Pour the hot broth over the noodles.

6. Garnish with sliced green onions and top with a soft-boiled egg.

7. Serve immediately and enjoy!

# MISO RAMEN

## Ingredients:

- Four packs of ramen noodles
- One tablespoon of vegetable oil
- 4 cups chicken or vegetable broth
- Two tablespoons of miso paste
- One tablespoon of soy sauce
- One tablespoon of sesame oil
- Toppings (optional): sliced green onions, soft-boiled eggs, sliced mushrooms, seaweed

## Instructions:

1. Prepare the ramen noodles as directed on the package. Empty and place aside.

2. Warm the vegetable oil in a big pot over medium heat. Add miso paste and cook for 1 minute, stirring constantly.

3. Add the broth and boil for a while. Stir in soy sauce and sesame oil.

4. Divide cooked ramen noodles into bowls. Ladle the hot broth over the noodles.

5. Add desired toppings such as green onions, soft-boiled eggs, mushrooms, or seaweed.

6. Serve immediately and enjoy your delicious miso ramen!

# TONKOTSU RAMEN

## Ingredients:

- 4-6 pork bones
- One onion, chopped
- Four cloves of garlic, minced
- 2 inches of ginger, sliced
- One tablespoon of vegetable oil
- 8 cups water
- 1 cup chicken broth
- Two tablespoons of soy sauce
- One tablespoon mirin (sweet rice wine)
- Salt and pepper to taste

## Instructions:

1. Fill a big pot with vegetable oil and heat it over medium heat. Add the chopped onion, minced garlic, and sliced ginger. Cook until fragrant.

2. Add the pork bones to the pot and simmer, stirring regularly, for approximately five minutes.

3. Pour in the water and chicken broth. After bringing to a boil, turn down the heat. Simmer for at least 4 hours, skimming off any impurities that float to the top.

4. Once the broth has simmered for several hours and reduced in volume, strain it into another pot or large bowl.

5. Return the strained broth to the stove and add soy sauce, mirin, salt, and pepper to taste. Simmer for an additional few minutes.

6. Cook your ramen noodles according to package instructions.

7. Serve your tonkatsu ramen by placing cooked noodles in a bowl and pouring hot broth. Top with desired garnishes like sliced cha shu pork, soft-boiled eggs, green onions, nori sheets, or bamboo shoots.

8. Enjoy your homemade tonkots.

# VEGETARIAN RAMEN

## Ingredients:

- Two tablespoons of soy sauce
- One tablespoon of miso paste
- One garlic clove, minced
- 1 inch ginger, grated
- Two green onions, sliced
- One carrot, julienned
- 1/2 cup mushrooms, sliced
- Two packs of ramen noodles

## Instructions:

1. Raise the chopped vegetable soup to a boil in a pot.

2. Add soy sauce, miso paste, garlic, and ginger to the broth and stir well.

3. Add in the green onions, carrots, and mushrooms. Let it simmer for about 5 minutes until the vegetables are tender.

4. Cook the ramen noodles separately according to package instructions.

5. Drain the cooked noodles and divide them into serving bowls.

6. Ladle the hot broth with vegetables over the noodles.

7. Serve immediately and enjoy your vegetarian ramen!

# SPICY TAN TAN MEN

## Ingredients:

- 300g ramen noodles
- 200g ground pork
- Two cloves garlic, minced
- One tablespoon ginger, grated
- One tablespoon of sesame oil
- Two tablespoons of soy sauce
- One tablespoon of chili garlic sauce
- 4 cups chicken broth
- Green onions, thinly sliced (for garnish)
- Soft-boiled eggs (optional)

## Instructions:

1. Prepare the ramen noodles as directed on the package. Empty and place aside.

2. In a large pot, heat sesame oil over medium heat. Add minced garlic and grated ginger, and sauté for 1 minute.

3. Add ground pork to the pot and cook until browned.

4. Stir in soy and chili garlic, mixing well with the pork.

5. Pour in chicken broth and bring to a simmer. Let it cook for about 10 minutes.

6. Divide cooked ramen noodles into bowls and ladle the spicy broth.

7. Garnish with sliced green onions and soft-boiled eggs if desired.

8. Serve hot and enjoy!

# SEAFOOD RAMEN

## Ingredients:

- 2 cups seafood broth
- One pack of ramen noodles
- 1 cup mixed seafood (shrimp, squid, mussels)
- Four cloves garlic, minced
- Two tablespoons of soy sauce
- One tablespoon of sesame oil
- Green onions for garnish

## Instructions:

1. In a pot, bring the seafood broth to a boil.

2. Add the minced garlic and soy sauce to the broth and let it simmer for a few minutes.

3. Cook the ramen noodles according to package instructions, then drain and set aside.

4. In a separate pan, heat the sesame oil and sauté the mixed seafood until cooked through.

5. Pour the broth over the cooked ramen noodles and top with sautéed seafood.

6. Add finely chopped green onions as a garnish and serve warm.

Enjoy your homemade Seafood Ramen!

# COLD RAMEN (HIYASHI CHUKA)

## Ingredients:

- Ramen noodles
- Cucumber
- Carrot
- Ham or chicken
- Eggs
- Soy sauce
- Rice vinegar
- Sesame oil
- Sugar
- Salt

## Instructions:

1. Prepare the ramen noodles per the directions on the package. Drain and rinse with cold water.

2. Julienne the cucumber, carrot, and ham or chicken.

3. Boil the eggs and slice them in half.

4. mix soy sauce, rice vinegar, sesame oil, sugar, and salt in a separate bowl to make the dressing.

5. Arrange the noodles on a plate and top with cucumber, carrot, ham or chicken, and boiled eggs.

6. Drizzle the dressing over the noodles and serve chilled.

# TSUKEMEN

## Ingredients:

- Ramen noodles
- Pork belly slices
- Spring onions
- Nori seaweed
- Soft-boiled eggs
- Tsukemen dipping sauce

## Instructions:

1. Prepare the ramen noodles per the directions on the package and set aside.

2. Grill pork belly slices until crispy and set aside.

3. Thinly slice spring onions and cut nori seaweed into small strips.

4. Soft-boil eggs and peel them.

5. Serve cooked ramen noodles in a bowl with grilled pork belly, spring onions, nori seaweed, and soft-boiled eggs on top.

6. Heat tsukemen dipping sauce and serve alongside the bowl of noodles for dipping. Enjoy!

# CHICKEN PAITAN RAMEN

## Ingredients:

- Two boneless, skinless chicken breasts
- 4 cups chicken broth
- Two cloves garlic, minced
- One tablespoon ginger, grated

- Two tablespoons of soy sauce
- Two tablespoons mirin (sweet rice wine)
- One teaspoon of sesame oil
- Two packs of ramen noodles
- Sliced green onions and soft-boiled eggs for garnish

## Instructions:

1. In a pot, bring the chicken broth to a boil.

2. Fill the pot with the grated ginger and minced garlic.

3. Add the chicken breasts to the boiling soup after chopping them into small pieces.

4. Stir in the soy sauce, mirin, and sesame oil.

5. Let the chicken cook for about 10 minutes until cooked through.

6. Cook the ramen noodles according to package instructions separately.

7. Drain the noodles and divide them among serving bowls.

8. Ladle the chicken broth with cooked chicken over the noodles.

9. Garnish with sliced green onions and soft-boiled eggs.

10. Serve hot, and enjoy your delicious Chicken pitaan ramen!

## SPICY KIMCHI RAMEN

## Ingredients:

- Two packs of instant ramen noodles
- 1 cup of kimchi
- One tablespoon of gochujang (Korean chili paste)
- One tablespoon of soy sauce

- Two green onions, sliced
- Two soft-boiled eggs, halved

## Instructions:

1. Prepare the ramen noodles per the directions on the back of the package, then drain and set aside.

2. heat some oil over medium heat in a separate pot and add the kimchi. Sauté for a few minutes until slightly softened.

3. Stir in the gochujang and soy sauce until well combined.

4. Add the cooked ramen noodles to the pot and whisk until the kimchi mixture coats the noodles.

5. Divide the ramen into bowls and top with sliced green onions and halved soft-boiled eggs.

6. Serve hot, and enjoy your spicy kimchi ramen!

# TEMPURA TREASURES

## SHRIMP TEMPURA

## Ingredients:

- 1 pound of shrimp, peeled and deveined
- 1 cup of all-purpose flour
- 1 cup of ice-cold water
- Vegetable oil for frying
- Salt to taste

## Instructions:

1. whisk the flour, salt, and ice-cold water in a mixing bowl until smooth.

2. Preheat a big pot or deep fryer to 375°F (190°C) using vegetable oil.

3. Dip each shrimp into the batter, coating it completely, and carefully place it into the hot oil.

4. Fry the shrimp for 2-3 minutes or until golden brown and crispy.

5. Remove the shrimp from the oil and drain on paper towels.

6. Repeat steps 3-5 for the remaining shrimp.

7. Serve immediately as an appetizer or main dish with your favorite dipping sauce.

# VEGETABLE TEMPURA

## Ingredients:

- Assorted vegetables (such as bell peppers, carrots, broccoli)
- Tempura batter mix
- Vegetable oil for frying

## Instructions:

1. Cut the vegetables into bite-sized pieces.

2. Prepare the tempura batter mix according to package instructions.

3. In a deep pan or fryer, preheat the vegetable oil.

4. Dip the vegetables into the tempura batter, ensuring they are fully coated.

5. Carefully place the battered vegetables into the hot oil and fry until golden brown.

6. Take out of the oil and let dry on paper towels.

7. Serve immediately as a first course or a side dish with your preferred dipping sauce. Enjoy!

# SWEET POTATO TEMPURA

## Ingredients:

- One large sweet potato
- 1 cup all-purpose flour
- 1 cup cold water
- Vegetable oil for frying

## Instructions:

1. Slice the sweet potato into thin

circles after peeling.

2. Mix flour and cold water to make a smooth batter in a mixing bowl.

1. After peeling, thinly slice the sweet potato into rings.

4. Dip each sweet potato slice into the batter, coating it evenly.

5. Gently drop the coated slices into the heated oil, frying them till crispy and golden brown.

6. To get rid of extra oil, take from oil and drain on paper towels.

7. Serve immediately as an appetizer or side dish with your favorite dipping sauce. Enjoy!

# TEMPURA UDON

## Ingredients:

- One package of udon noodles
- 1 cup all-purpose flour
- 1 cup ice cold water
- One egg
- Assorted vegetables (such as carrots, bell peppers, and zucchini)
- Vegetable oil for frying

## Instructions:

1. Prepare the udon noodles as directed on the packet. Drain and set aside.

2. In a bowl, whisk together flour, ice-cold water, and egg until smooth.

3. preheat the vegetable oil in a deep pan or saucepan before frying.

4. Dip the vegetables in the batter, coating evenly.

5. Fry the vegetables in hot oil until golden brown and crispy.

6. To absorb any remaining oil, remove the fried vegetables from the oil and place them on paper towels.

7. Divide the cooked udon noodles into serving bowls.

8. Pour hot tempura sauce over the noodles.

9. Top with fried vegetables and serve immediately.

# TEMPURA SOBA

## Ingredients:

- Soba noodles
- Tempura batter mix
- Assorted vegetables (such as carrots, zucchini, and bell peppers)
- Vegetable oil for frying
- Tempura dipping sauce

## Instructions:

1. Prepare the soba noodles per the directions on the package. Empty and place aside.

2. Prepare tempura batter mix according to package instructions.

3. Slice vegetables into thin strips or bite-sized pieces.

4. Preheat a deep pan or pot with vegetable oil for frying.

5. Dip vegetables into the tempura batter, ensuring they are well coated.

6. Gently drop the battered veggies into the heated oil and cook them until they are crispy and golden brown.

7. Remove the fried veggies from the oil and put them on a platter covered with paper towels to absorb extra oil.

8. Serve soba noodles in bowls, topped with the crispy tempura vegetables.

9. Serve with tempura dipping sauce on the side for dipping the vegetables and noodles.

**Note:** This recipe can be customized if desired by adding protein such as shrimp or tofu to the tempura mix.

# KAKIAGE TEMPURA

## Ingredients:

- 1 cup all-purpose flour
- 1 cup ice-cold water
- One small onion, thinly sliced
- One carrot, julienned
- One zucchini, thinly sliced
- Vegetable oil for frying

## Instructions:

1. whisk the flour and ice-cold water together until smooth.

2. Preheat 350°F (175°C) vegetable oil in a deep fryer or large pot.

3. Dip the onion, carrot juliennes, and zucchini slices into the batter, ensuring they are well coated.

4. Fry the vegetables until golden brown and crispy, about 2-3 minutes per batch.

5. Using a slotted spoon, remove and place on paper towels to drain.

6. Serve hot as an appetizer or rice as a main dish. Enjoy!

# ANAGO TEMPURA

## Ingredients:

- Anago (saltwater eel)
- Tempura batter mix
- Vegetable oil for frying

## Instructions:

1. Slice the anago into bite-sized pieces.

2. Prepare the tempura batter mix according to package instructions.

3. prepare the vegetable oil in a deep pan or saucepan while frying.

4. Dip each piece of anago into the tempura batter, coating it evenly.

5. Gently drop the battered pieces into the heated oil and cook them until they are crispy and golden brown.

6. Remove from the oil and drain excess grease on a paper towel.

7. Serve hot and enjoy!

## MOCHIKO CHICKEN TEMPURA

### Ingredients:

- One pound of chicken breast, sliced into small pieces
- 1 cup mochiko (sweet rice flour)
- 1/2 cup cornstarch
- 1/4 cup soy sauce
- Two tablespoons sugar
- One tablespoon of sesame oil
- Vegetable oil for frying

### Instructions:

1. combine mochiko, cornstarch, soy sauce, sugar, and sesame oil in a bowl. Mix well.

2. Transfer the chicken pieces to the bowl and coat them with the mixture.

3. In a deep pan or fryer, heat the vegetable oil over medium-high heat.

4. Gently slide the coated chicken into the heated oil and cook it for five to seven minutes or until it is cooked through and golden brown.

5. After removing the chicken from the oil, pat dry using paper towels.

6. Serve hot and enjoy!

# PUMPKIN TEMPURA

## Ingredients:

- One small pumpkin
- 1 cup all-purpose flour
- One teaspoon of baking powder
- 1/2 teaspoon salt
- 1 cup ice-cold water
- Vegetable oil for frying

## Instructions:

1. Cut the pumpkin into thin slices.

2. In an immense bowl, whisk combined flour, cocoa powder, baking soda, and salt.

3. Add cold water to the dry ingredients, whisking until smooth.

4. In a deep pan or saucepan, heat the vegetable oil over medium-high heat.

5. Dip each pumpkin slice into the batter and coat evenly.

6. Carefully drop the battered pumpkin slices into the heated oil, cooking them for about two minutes on each side or until golden brown.

7. Remove from the oil and place on paper towels to drain.

8. Serve immediately as a crispy and delicious appetizer or snack. Enjoy!

# MUSHROOM TEMPURA

## Ingredients:

- 8 ounces of mushrooms
- 1/2 cup of all-purpose flour
- 1/2 cup of cold sparkling water
- Vegetable oil for frying
- Salt and pepper to taste

## Instructions:

1. Clean the mushrooms and slice them into thin pieces.

2. In a bowl, mix the flour, sparkling water, salt, and pepper until smooth.

3. warm the vegetable oil over medium-high heat in a big skillet or pot.

4. Dip each mushroom slice into the batter, allowing any excess to drip off.

5. Gently drop the battered mushrooms into the heated oil and cook them in batches until they are crispy and golden brown.

6. Utilizing a slotted spoon, withdraw from the oil and place it on a plate topped with towels made of paper to drain excess fat.

7. Serve immediately as an appetizer or side dish with your favorite dipping sauce. Enjoy!

# IZAKAYA EATS
## YAKITORI

### Ingredients:

- 1 pound boneless, skinless chicken thighs
- 1/4 cup soy sauce
- 1/4 cup mirin (sweet rice wine)
- Two tablespoons sugar
- Two tablespoons sake (Japanese rice wine)
- Bamboo skewers

### Instructions:

1. Roughly chop the chicken thighs into small pieces.

2. mix the soy sauce, mirin, sugar, and sake in a bowl to make the marinade.

3. Place the chicken pieces in the marinade and let them marinate for at least 30 minutes.

4. Preheat your grill or broiler.

5. Thread the marinated chicken onto bamboo skewers.

6. Grill or broil the skewers on each side for 3-4 minutes until cooked and slightly charred.

7. Serve hot as an appetizer or with steamed rice as a main dish. Enjoy!

# OKONOMIYAKI

## Ingredients:

- 2 cups shredded cabbage
- 1 cup all-purpose flour
- 1/2 cup water
- Two eggs
- 1/4 cup chopped green onions
- 1/4 cup bonito flakes (optional)
- 1/4 cup mayonnaise
- 1/4 cup okonomiyaki sauce or Worcestershire sauce
- Vegetable oil for frying

## Instructions:

1. mix the cabbage, flour, water, eggs, and green onions until well combined in a large bowl.

2. In a nonstick skillet, preheat a small amount of vegetable oil over medium heat.

3. Transfer roughly half of the batter to the skillet and flatten it into a circular shape.

4. Cook for 3 minutes on each side until golden brown and crispy.

5. Continue to make more okonomiyaki pancakes with the leftover batter.

6. Serve hot, topped with mayonnaise, okonomiyaki sauce, or Worcestershire sauce, and sprinkle with bonito flakes if desired. Enjoy!

# TAKOYAKI

## Ingredients:

- 2 cups all-purpose flour
- Two teaspoons of baking powder
- 1/2 teaspoon salt
- Two tablespoons of soy sauce
- Two eggs
- 1 cup water
- 1 cup chopped cooked octopus (tako)
- Green onions, thinly sliced (for garnish)
- Takoyaki sauce (optional)
- Japanese mayonnaise (optional)

## Instructions:

1. In a mixing container, mix together flour, baking powder, and salt.

2. Add soy sauce, eggs, and water to the mixture and stir until smooth.

3. Heat a takoyaki pan over medium heat and brush each mold with oil.

4. Pour batter into each mold until half full.

5. Place a piece of chopped octopus in each mold and top with more batter to cover.

6. Cook for about 3 minutes or until golden brown on the bottom.

7. Using a skewer or chopsticks, flip the takoyaki balls over and cook for 3 minutes or until cooked.

8. Transfer takoyaki to a serving plate and garnish with green onions.

9. Drizzle with takoyaki sauce and Japanese mayonnaise if desired.

10. Serve hot and enjoy!

# EDAMAME

## Ingredients:

- 1 cup frozen edamame
- One tablespoon of olive oil
- Salt to taste

## Instructions:

1. Add the frozen edamame to a pot of boiling water.

2. Cook for 5-7 minutes or until edamame is tender.

3. Drain and rinse the edamame under cold water.

4. Medium the tablespoon of olive oil in a skillet over medium heat.

5. Add the cooked edamame to the skillet and sauté for 2-3 minutes.

6. Sprinkle with salt, toss to coat, and serve hot. Enjoy!

# GYOZA

## Ingredients:

- One package of gyoza wrappers
- 1/2-pound ground pork
- 1 cup shredded cabbage
- Two cloves garlic, minced
- One tablespoon ginger, grated
- Two tablespoons of soy sauce
- One tablespoon of sesame oil

## Instructions:

1. In a serving dish, incorporate the ground pork, sesame oil, soy sauce, ginger, garlic, and cabbage.

2. Spoon about a teaspoon of the filling onto each gyoza wrapper.

3. Warm up the outer edges inside the wrapping with water and fold it in half to generate a half-moon.

4. Press the edges firmly to seal the gyoza.

5. Add the gyoza to a pan with hot oil over medium heat.

6. Cook for about 2 minutes until the bottom turns golden brown.

7. Pour about 1/4 cup of water into the pan and cover it immediately with a lid.

8. Steam for approximately five minutes or until the wrappers are transparent and the contents are cooked.

9. Take off the heat source and accompany it with a warm dipping sauce. Enjoy!

# EBI MAYO

## Ingredients:

- 12 large shrimp, peeled and deveined
- 1/2 cup mayonnaise
- One tablespoon of Sriracha sauce
- One tablespoon of soy sauce
- One teaspoon honey
- Vegetable oil for frying

## Instructions:

1. mix the mayonnaise, Sriracha sauce, soy sauce, and honey until well combined.

2. Preheat a deep pan or fryer to 350°F (175°C) using vegetable oil.

3. Dip the shrimp into the mayo mixture until coated evenly.

4. Gently drop the coated shrimp into the heated oil, frying them for about two minutes on each side or until golden brown.

5. Remove from heat and drain on paper towels.

6. Serve hot and enjoy your delicious Ebi Mayo!

## KARAAGE

## Ingredients:

- Boneless chicken thighs
- Soy sauce
- Mirin (Japanese sweet rice wine)
- Garlic
- Ginger
- Cornstarch
- Vegetable oil for frying

## Instructions:

1. Cut the boneless chicken thighs into bite-sized pieces.

2. combine soy sauce, mirin, minced garlic, and grated ginger as marinade in a bowl.

3. Add chicken pieces to the marinade and let it marinate for at least 30 minutes.

4. Heat vegetable oil in a deep-frying pan or pot.

5. Coat marinated chicken pieces with cornstarch.

6. Fry the coated chicken in hot oil until golden brown and crispy.

7. Take out of the oil and let dry on paper towels.

8. Enjoy hot, either by itself or with your preferred dipping sauce!

## YAKI UDON

### Ingredients:

- Udon noodles
- Vegetable oil
- Garlic
- Onion
- Bell pepper
- Carrot
- Cabbage leaves
- Soy sauce
- Mirin (Japanese sweet rice wine)
- Salt and pepper

### Instructions:

1. Prepare the udon pasta per the directions on the back of the package, then drain and set aside.

2. In a big sauce pan or wok, warm the oil made of coconut over medium heat.

3. Add minced garlic, diced onion, sliced bell pepper, julienned carrot, and shredded cabbage leaves to the skillet. Stir-fry for a few minutes until vegetables are slightly softened.

4. Push the vegetables to one side of the skillet and add the cooked udon noodles to the other side.

5. Cover the noodles with a drizzle of soy sauce and mirin, and season without a bit of pepper and salt.

6. Toss everything together until well combined and heated through.

7. Serve hot as a delicious Yaki Udon dish!

# TEBASAKI

## Ingredients:

- 2 pounds of chicken wings
- 1 cup of soy sauce
- 1/2 cup of mirin (Japanese rice wine)
- 1/4 cup of sake (Japanese rice wine)
- Two tablespoons of sugar
- Two cloves of garlic, minced
- One teaspoon of grated ginger

## Instructions:

1. Set the oven's temperature to 425°F (220°C).

2. combine soy sauce, mirin, sake, sugar, garlic, and ginger in a saucepan. Bring to a simmer over medium heat.

3. Place chicken wings in a baking dish and pour the sauce over them.

4. Bake for approximately 25 minutes or until the chicken is cooked through and golden brown.

5. Serve hot, and enjoy your Tebasaki!

# AGE-DASHI TOFU

## Ingredients:

- One package of firm tofu
- Two tablespoons cornstarch
- Vegetable oil for frying
- 1 cup dashi stock
- Two tablespoons of soy sauce
- One tablespoon mirin
- Green onions, chopped (for garnish)

## Instructions:

1. Cut the tofu into bite-sized cubes and pat dry with paper towels.

2. Coat the tofu cubes in cornstarch until fully coated.

3. In a deep pan or fryer, heat the onion and garlic oil over medium-high heat.

4. Fry the tofu cubes until golden brown and crispy on all sides. Drain on paper towels.

5. bring dashi stock, soy sauce, and mirin to a boil in a separate saucepan.

6. Reduce heat and simmer for 2-3 minutes.

7. Pour the sauce over the fried tofu cubes.

8. Garnish with chopped green onions.

9. Serve hot as an appetizer or side dish with steamed rice or noodles. Enjoy!

# BENTO BOX BONANZA

## Ingredients:

- Teriyaki Chicken Bento
- Two chicken breasts
- 1/4 cup soy sauce
- 1/4 cup mirin
- Two tablespoons brown sugar
- One tablespoon of sesame oil
- One garlic clove, minced
- One teaspoon of grated ginger
- Cooked white rice
- Steamed broccoli and carrots (optional)
- Sesame seeds for garnish

## Instructions:

1. Mix a bowl of soy sauce, mirin, brown sugar, sesame oil, garlic, and ginger.

2. Cut chicken breasts into bite-sized pieces and marinate in the sauce for at least 30 minutes.

3. Toast the marinated chicken in a pan over medium heat until it's cooked and has a hint of caramelization.

4. Divide cooked rice into bento boxes or meal prep containers.

5. Add steamed broccoli and carrots (if desired) to the bento boxes.

6. Place the cooked teriyaki chicken on top of the rice.

7. Sprinkle with sesame seeds for garnish.

8. Serve immediately or refrigerate for later consumption.

# SUSHI BENTO

## Ingredients:

- Cooked sushi rice
- Nori (seaweed sheets)
- Sliced raw fish or cooked seafood
- Fresh vegetables (cucumber, carrots, avocado)
- Soy sauce
- Wasabi
- Pickled ginger

## Instructions:

1. Set up the nori sheet on a type of sushi mat made of bamboo.

2. Evenly cover the nori with a thin layer of sushi rice.

3. Place your choice of sliced raw fish or cooked seafood in the center of the rice.

4. Add thinly sliced vegetables on top.

5. Carefully roll the sushi using the bamboo mat, pressing gently to ensure it holds its shape.

6. Slice the sushi roll into bite-sized pieces.

7. Serve with soy sauce, wasabi, and pickled ginger on the side for dipping. Enjoy your sushi bento!

# BEEF YAKINIKU BENTO

## Ingredients:

- 1 pound thinly sliced beef
- 1/4 cup soy sauce
- Two tablespoons sugar
- Two tablespoons mirin (sweet rice wine)
- One tablespoon of sesame oil
- Two garlic cloves, minced
- One teaspoon of grated ginger
- Cooked white rice
- Assorted vegetables (such as bell peppers, mushrooms, and onions)

## Instructions:

1. combine soy sauce, sugar, mirin, sesame oil, garlic cloves, and grated ginger in a bowl.

2. Marinate the beef slices in the sauce for at least 30 minutes.

3. Turn up the heat to medium-high on a grill or skillet.

4. Cook the marinated beef slices for about 2 minutes on each side until browned and cooked through.

5. Remove the beef from the heat and set aside.

6. In the same pan, stir-fry the assorted vegetables until crisp-tender.

7. Divide cooked white rice into bento boxes or containers.

8. Arrange cooked beef slices and stir-fried vegetables on the rice.

9. Serve hot or cold as a delicious Beef Yakiniku Bento meal!

# EEL KABAYAKI BENTO

## Ingredients:

- Two eel fillets
- Two tablespoons of soy sauce
- Two tablespoons mirin (sweet rice wine)
- One tablespoon sugar

## Instructions:

1. Preheat grill or broiler.

2. mix sugar, mirin, and soy sauce in a small saucepan. Simmer the sugar under a medium-high flame until it melts.

3. Brush eel fillets with the sauce mixture.

4. Grill or broil eel fillets for about 5 minutes on each side, brushing with sauce occasionally.

5. Serve the grilled eel on steamed rice in a bento box.

# TEMPURA BENTO

## Ingredients:

- Tempura batter mix
- Vegetables (such as broccoli, carrots, and bell peppers)
- Seafood or protein of choice (shrimp, fish, chicken, tofu)
- Vegetable oil for frying
- Cooked rice
- Soy sauce
- Pickled ginger
- Nori seaweed sheets

## Instructions:

1. Prepare the tempura batter mix according to the package instructions.

2. thinly slice the protein and chop the veggies into bite-sized pieces if necessary.

3. In a deep pan or pot, preheat the vegetable oil.

4. After dipping the protein and veggies in the tempura batter, carefully drop them into the heated oil and cook until crispy and golden brown.

5. Take out the oil and pat dry with paper towels.

6. Divide cooked rice into sections in a bento box or plate.

7. Arrange the tempura vegetables and protein in the rice sections.

8. Serve with soy sauce for dipping, pickled ginger for added flavor, and nori seaweed sheets for garnish if desired.

9. Enjoy your delicious tempura bento!

# PORK KATSU BENTO

## Ingredients:
- Pork cutlets
- Panko breadcrumbs
- Flour
- Eggs
- Salt and pepper
- Vegetable oil

## Instructions:

1. Use salt and pepper to season the pork cutlets on both sides.

2. Coat each cutlet in flour, dip them in beaten eggs, and coat them with panko breadcrumbs.

3. In the bottom of a frying pan, temperature the vegetable oil over medium heat.

4. Fry the breaded pork cutlets until golden brown and cooked through, about 5 minutes per side.

5. Take out of the pan and lay to absorb any remaining oil on a paper towel.

6. Slice the cooked pork cutlets into bite-sized pieces.

7. Serve with steamed rice, shredded cabbage, and tonkatsu sauce in a bento box or plate. Enjoy your Pork Katsu Bento!

# TSUKUNE BENTO

## Ingredients:

- 500g ground chicken
- Two green onions, finely chopped
- Two cloves garlic, minced
- 1/4 cup panko breadcrumbs
- Two tablespoons of soy sauce
- One tablespoon mirin (sweet rice wine)
- One tablespoon of sesame oil
- Salt and pepper to taste
- Bamboo skewers

## Instructions:

1. combine ground chicken, green onions, garlic, panko breadcrumbs, soy sauce, mirin, sesame oil, salt, and pepper in a mixing bowl.

2. Thoroughly stir until all items are combined.

3. Form the ingredients into small oval-shaped meatballs by dividing them into pieces.

4. Thread each meatball onto a bamboo skewer.

5. Preheat a grill or broiler on medium heat.

6. Cook the meatballs for about 8-10 minutes, turning occasionally until they are cooked and nicely browned.

7. Remove from heat and let them cool slightly before packing them in your bento box along with desired sides like rice, vegetables, and pickles.

8. Enjoy your delicious Tsukune Bento!

## OYAKODON BENTO

### Ingredients:
- 2 cups cooked rice
- One chicken breast, thinly sliced
- One onion, thinly sliced
- Three eggs, beaten
- Two tablespoons of soy sauce
- One tablespoon mirin (sweet rice wine)
- One tablespoon sugar
- Green onions, chopped for garnish

### Instructions:
1. Cook the chicken in a big skillet over medium heat until it turns no longer pink.

2. Cook the onion until it becomes tender.

3. mix soy sauce, mirin, and sugar in a small bowl.

4. Add the marinade to the skillet and let it simmer for a short while...

5. Pour beaten eggs evenly over the chicken and onion mixture in the skillet.

6. Cover and cook on low heat until eggs are set.

7. Serve the oyakodon over a bed of rice in a bento box and garnish with chopped green onions.

8. Enjoy your delicious oyakodon bento!

## SHRIMP AND VEGETABLE BENTO

### Ingredients:

- 1 cup cooked shrimp
- 1 cup cooked brown rice
- 1 cup steamed broccoli
- 1/2 cup sliced carrots
- 1/2 cup sliced bell peppers
- Two tablespoons of soy sauce
- One tablespoon of sesame oil

### Instructions:

1. mix the shrimp, rice, broccoli, carrots, and bell peppers in a large bowl.

2. Drizzle with soy sauce and sesame oil.

3. Toss to coat everything evenly.

4. Divide the mixture into individual bento boxes or containers.

5. Serve chilled or at room temperature for a delicious and healthy meal!

# TOFU STEAK BENTO

## Ingredients:

- One block of firm tofu
- Two tablespoons of soy sauce
- One tablespoon of sesame oil
- One tablespoon of rice vinegar
- One teaspoon of garlic powder
- One teaspoon of ginger powder
- Salt and pepper to taste
- Cooked rice
- Assorted vegetables (carrots, cucumber, bell peppers, etc.)
- Nori seaweed sheets

## Instructions:

1. Slice the tofu into steak-sized pieces after pressing it to remove more water.

2. Mix in a shallow dish in soy sauce, sesame oil, rice vinegar, garlic powder, ginger powder, salt, and pepper.

3. Marinate tofu in the mixture for at least 15 minutes.

4. Cook tofu steaks in a nonstick pan over medium heat for 5 minutes on each side or until browned.

5. Arrange cooked rice, tofu steaks, and assorted vegetables in a bento box or plate.

6. Decorate with nori seaweed sheets if desired.

7. Enjoy your delicious Tofu Steak Bento!

# JAPANESE COMFORT SOUPS

## MISO SOUP

### Ingredients:

- 4 cups vegetable broth
- Two tablespoons of miso paste
- 1 cup tofu, cubed
- 1 cup mushrooms, sliced
- Two green onions, chopped

### Instructions:

1. In a pot, bring vegetable broth to a boil.

2. Combine miso paste and a small amount of boiling broth in a small bowl and whisk until smooth.

3. Add the miso mixture to the pot and stir well.

4. Add tofu and mushrooms to the pot and simmer for 5 minutes.

5. Add green onions as a garnish and serve hot. Enjoy!

## CLEAR SOUP

### Ingredients:

- 1 onion
- 2 carrots
- 2 celery stalks
- 4 cups vegetable broth
- Salt and pepper to taste

## Instructions:

1. Finely chop the celery, carrots, and onion.

2. Sauté the chopped vegetables in a pot with a little oil over medium heat for 5 minutes.

3. Include the veggie broth and bring the mixture to a boil.

4.Wait for 20 minutes while the pot is covered and the heat is lowered to a simmer.

5. To taste, add salt and pepper to the food.

6. Serve the clear soup hot.

# CHAWANMUSHI

## Ingredients:

- Two large eggs
- 1 cup chicken stock
- One tablespoon of soy sauce
- One teaspoon mirin (sweet rice wine)
- Two shiitake mushrooms, sliced
- Two tablespoons of corn kernels
- Two green onions, chopped

## Instructions:

1. whisk together eggs, chicken stock, soy sauce, and mirin in a bowl.

2. Place mushroom slices and corn kernels in the bottom of heatproof cups or bowls.

3. Pour the egg mixture over the mushrooms and corn.

4. Steam the cups or bowls over medium heat for about 10 minutes or until the custard is set but still slightly jiggly in the center.

5. Garnish with chopped green onions before serving. Enjoy Chawanmushi warm or chilled!

# ODEN

## Ingredients:

- 4 cups dashi broth
- 1 cup soy sauce
- Two tablespoons mirin
- One tablespoon sugar
- Assorted Oden ingredients (e.g., daikon radish, konnyaku, boiled eggs, fish cakes)
- Green onions for garnish

## Instructions:

1. combine dashi broth, soy sauce, mirin, and sugar in a pot.

2. Bring the mixture to a boil.

3. Add the oden ingredients to the pot.

4. Simmer on low heat for about 30 minutes or until the ingredients are cooked through and tender.

5. Serve hot in bowls, garnished with green onions.

6. Enjoy your homemade oden!

# ZONI

## Ingredients:

- 6 cups dashi (Japanese soup stock)
- 1/4 cup soy sauce
- Two tablespoons mirin (sweet rice wine)
- One teaspoon salt
- 1 pound boneless pork belly, sliced
- Four mochis (rice cakes), toasted
- Four green onions, chopped
- Four sheets of nori (seaweed), cut into thin strips

## Instructions:

1. In a pot, bring the dashi to a boil.

2. Add soy sauce, mirin, and salt to the pot.

3. Add sliced pork belly and simmer for 10 minutes.

4. Take out and set aside the pork from the pot.

5. Divide the cooked pork, toasted mochi, green onions, and nori strips into four serving bowls.

6. Ladle hot broth over the ingredients in each bowl.

7. Serve immediately and enjoy your zone!

# TONJIRU

## Ingredients:

- 500g pork belly
- One onion
- Three carrots
- Two potatoes
- One daikon radish
- Four shiitake mushrooms
- Two tablespoons of miso paste

## Instructions:

1. Slice the pork belly into thin strips.

2. Chop the onion, carrots, potatoes, daikon radish, and mushrooms into bite-sized pieces.

3. In a large pot, cook the pork belly until browned.

4. Cook the chopped veggies in the pot for a short while.

5. Dissolve miso paste in water and add it to the pot.

6. Add enough water to cover the contents in the pot and bring it to a boil.

7. Reduce heat and simmer for 30 minutes or until vegetables are tender.

8. Serve hot and enjoy Tonjiru!

# NIKUJAGA

## Ingredients:

- 500g beef slices
- Four potatoes, peeled and cut into chunks
- Two carrots, sliced
- One onion, thinly sliced
- 3 cups dashi stock
- Three tablespoons soy sauce
- Two tablespoons sugar
- One tablespoon mirin (Japanese sweet rice wine)

## Instructions:

1. Heat some oil in a big pot and sauté the onions until they are transparent.

2. Add the beef slices and cook until browned.

3. Include the carrots and potatoes in the pot.

4. Pour in the dashi stock, soy sauce, sugar, and mirin.

5. After bringing to a boil, lower the heat, and simmer the potatoes until they are soft, about 20 minutes.

6. Serve hot with steamed rice. Enjoy!

# SUMASHI JIRU

## Ingredients:

- 4 cups dashi broth
- One tablespoon of soy sauce
- One tablespoon mirin

- One teaspoon salt
- Two green onions, chopped
- Eight shiitake mushrooms, sliced
- Optional: tofu, sliced

## Instructions:

1. In a pot, bring the dashi broth to a simmer.

2. Add soy sauce, mirin, and salt. Stir well.

3. Add green onions and shiitake mushrooms (and tofu if desired).

4. Simmer for about 5 minutes until mushrooms are tender.

5. Serve hot and enjoy!

# DOJO NABE

## Ingredients:

- 500g thinly sliced beef
- One pack of enoki mushrooms
- Two groups of shimeji mushrooms
- One group of oyster mushrooms
- One block of tofu cubed
- 4 cups of dashi stock
- Two tablespoons of soy sauce
- Two tablespoons sake (Japanese rice wine)
- Two tablespoons mirin (sweet rice wine)
- Salt and pepper to taste

## Instructions:

1. heat the dashi stock over medium heat in a large pot.

2. Add soy sauce, sake, and mirin to the pot and boil.

3. Add the thinly sliced beef to the pot and cook until slightly browned.

4. Add the tofu and all the mushrooms to the pot and simmer for about 5 minutes.

5. Add pepper and salt to taste.

6. Serve hot in individual bowls and enjoy!

# TAKENOKO SOUP

## Ingredients:

- 2 cups sliced bamboo shoots
- 1 cup diced carrots
- 1 cup diced mushrooms
- 1 cup diced onions
- 4 cups vegetable broth
- Two tablespoons of soy sauce
- One tablespoon of sesame oil
- Salt and pepper to taste

## Instructions:

1. Heat the sesame oil in a big pot over medium heat.

2. Add onions and sauté until translucent.

3. Add carrots and mushrooms and cook for another 2 minutes.

4. Add the veggie broth and heat until it boils.

5. Stir in bamboo shoots and soy sauce; reduce heat to low.

6. Simmer the vegetables until they are soft, about 15 minutes.

7. To taste, add salt and pepper for seasoning.

8. Serve hot and enjoy!

# DONBURI DELIGHTS

## OYAKODON

**Ingredients:**

- Two boneless, skinless chicken breasts
- One onion
- Three eggs
- 1 cup dashi stock
- Two tablespoons of soy sauce
- Two tablespoons mirin (sweet rice wine)
- Cooked rice

**Instructions:**

1. Slice the chicken breasts and onion into thin strips.

2. combine dashi stock, soy sauce, and mirin in a pan. Bring to a simmer.

3. Add chicken and onion to the pan until the chicken is cooked through.

4. Gently beat the eggs in another bowl.

5. Pour the beaten eggs over the chicken and onion mixture in the pan.

6. Cover the pan and cook for a few minutes until the eggs are set.

7. Serve oyakodon over cooked rice and enjoy!

# GYUDON

## Ingredients:

- 1 pound thinly sliced beef
- One onion, thinly sliced
- Two tablespoons of soy sauce
- Two tablespoons mirin
- Two tablespoons sake
- One tablespoon sugar
- 1 cup beef broth

## Instructions:

1. Heat the oil in a big skillet over medium heat.

2. Add onions and cook until softened.

3. Add beef slices and cook until browned.

4. mix soy sauce, mirin, sake, sugar, and beef broth in a bowl.

5. Transfer the mixture to the skillet and let briefly for a short while.

6. Serve over steamed rice, and enjoy!

# KATSUDON

## Ingredients:

- Four boneless pork chops
- 1 cup panko breadcrumbs
- Two eggs, beaten
- 1/2 cup all-purpose flour
- Vegetable oil for frying

- One onion, sliced
- 4 cups cooked Japanese rice
- Four tablespoons of soy sauce
- Four tablespoons mirin (sweet rice wine)
- 2 cups dashi stock (or chicken broth)
- Four green onions, chopped

## Instructions:

1. Pound the pork chops until they are evenly thin.

2. Dip each pork chop in flour, then dip in beaten eggs and coat with panko bread source, grill the pork chops until they're golden brow side in a skillet containing heated oil from a vegetable source heir sides. Put away.

4. In the same pan, sauté sliced onions until softened.

5. Add soy sauce, mirin, and dashi stock to the pan and let it simmer for a few minutes.

6. Place the fried pork chops on top of the onion mixture in the pan.

7. Cook, covered, over low heat for five minutes or until the flavors are blended.

8. Serve hot cooked Japanese rice and garnish with chopped green onions.

## TENDON

## Ingredients:

- 2 pounds of beef tendon
- One onion, sliced
- Four cloves garlic, minced
- 1 cup soy sauce
- 1 cup water

- 1/2 cup brown sugar

## Instructions:

1. combine the beef tendon, onion, garlic, soy sauce, water, and brown sugar in a large pot.

2. Place the mixture on high heat and bring it to a boil.

3. Simmer the tendon for three hours, or until it is tender, on low heat.

4. Remove the tendon from the pot and let it cool.

5. Once cooled, slice the tendon into thin pieces.

6. Serve the tendon with rice or noodles, and enjoy!

## UNADON

### Ingredients:

- 1 cup unagi (eel), grilled and sliced
- 1/4 cup soy sauce
- 1/4 cup mirin (sweet rice wine)
- One tablespoon sugar
- 2 cups steamed white rice

### Instructions:

1. combine soy sauce, mirin, and sugar in a small saucepan. Heat the added sugar over medium heat until it dissolves.

2. Add the grilled eel slices to the saucepan and simmer for a few minutes until heated.

3. Serve the eel and sauce over steamed white rice.

4. Enjoy your delicious Unadon!

# TEKKADON

## Ingredients:

- Sushi rice
- Tuna sashimi
- Soy sauce
- Sesame oil
- Green onions

## Instructions:

1. Prepare the sushi rice per the directions on the package.

2. Cut tuna into bite-sized pieces.

3. In a bowl, mix soy sauce and sesame oil.

4. Place sushi rice in a bowl and top with tuna.

5. Drizzle the tuna and rice with the soy sauce mixture.

6. Garnish with chopped green onions.

# KAISENDON

## Ingredients:

- Sushi rice
- Raw fish (salmon, tuna, etc.)
- Avocado
- Cucumber
- Carrot
- Soy sauce
- Wasabi

## Instructions:

1. Prepare the sushi rice per the directions on the package.

2. Slice raw fish into thin strips.

3. Dice avocado, cucumber, and carrot.

4. Place a bed of sushi rice in a bowl.

5. Arrange sliced fish, avocado, cucumber, and carrot on the rice.

6. Serve with soy sauce and wasabi on the side.

7. Enjoy your Kaisendon!

## TOFU DON

## Ingredients:

- One block of tofu
- 2 cups of cooked rice
- 1 cup of sliced mushrooms
- 1 cup of sliced bell peppers
- 1/4 cup of soy sauce
- Two tablespoons of sesame oil
- Two tablespoons of cornstarch

## Instructions:

1. Drain and squeeze the tofu to get rid of extra water.

2. Cut the tofu into cubes.

3. In a bowl, mix soy sauce, sesame oil, and cornstarch to make a sauce.

4. Add the tofu cubes to a pan heated to medium heat.

5. Cook until all sides are golden brown.

6. Add mushrooms and bell peppers to the pan and cook for a few minutes.

7. Drizzle the tofu and veggies with the sauce, then gently toss to coat everything.

8. Serve the tofu mixture over cooked rice. Enjoy your Tofu Don!

# BUTADON

## Ingredients:
- 1 cup of short-grain rice
- 1/2 pound of thinly sliced pork belly
- Three tablespoons of soy sauce
- One tablespoon of mirin (Japanese sweet rice wine)
- One tablespoon of sugar
- Two green onions, sliced

## Instructions:
1. Prepare the rice as directed on the packet.

2. Cook the pork belly slices in a different pan until brown and crispy.

3. Mix confectioner's sugar, mirin, and soy sauce in a tiny bowl until dissolved.

4. Pour the sauce over the pork belly and let it simmer for a few minutes.

5. Place a serving of cooked rice in a bowl and top it with the pork belly slices and sauce.

6. Add sliced green onions as a garnish and serve hot.

# GOMOKU KAMAMESHI

## Ingredients:

- 1 cup Japanese short-grain rice
- 2 cups water
- One carrot, diced
- 1/2 cup snap peas, trimmed and halved
- 1/2 cup shiitake mushrooms, sliced
- 1/2 cup chicken or tofu, diced
- Two tablespoons of soy sauce
- One tablespoon mirin
- One tablespoon sake
- Optional toppings: sliced green onions, sesame seeds

## Instructions:

1. Wash the rice in cold water until clear.

2. In a large pot, combine the rinsed rice and water. Bring to a boil over high heat.

3. After the saucepan reaches a boil, turn down the heat and cover it. Cook for about 12 minutes or until the rice is tender.

4. Heat some oil in a different skillet and cook the chicken or tofu, snap peas, carrots, and mushrooms until they are well done.

5. Mix soy sauce, mirin, and sake in a small bowl.

6. Add the cooked vegetables and protein to the pot of cooked rice. Pour in the soy sauce mixture and gently stir everything together.

7. Cover the pot again and cook for 5 minutes on low heat to allow flavors to meld.

8. Serve hot with optional toppings like sliced green onions and sesame seeds.

9. Enjoy your Gomoku Kamameshi!

# JAPANESE NOODLES
## SOBA

**Ingredients:**

- 8 ounces of soba noodles
- Two tablespoons of soy sauce
- One tablespoon of sesame oil
- One teaspoon of rice vinegar
- One teaspoon honey
- 1/4 cup green onions, chopped
- 1/4 cup cilantro, chopped

**Instructions:**

1. Prepare the soba noodles as directed on the package, then rinse and drain under cold water.

2. Combine the soy sauce, sesame oil, honey, and rice vinegar in a small bowl.

3. Toss the cooked soba noodles with the sauce until evenly coated.

4. Garnish with green onions and cilantro before serving. Enjoy!

# UDON

## Ingredients:

- Udon noodles
- Broth (chicken or vegetable)
- Soy sauce
- Mirin (sweet Japanese rice wine)
- Toppings (optional: sliced green onions, tempura flakes, nori seaweed)

## Instructions:

1. Cook udon noodles according to package instructions and set aside.

2. In a pot, heat broth and bring to a simmer.

3. Add soy sauce and mirin to taste for flavoring.

4. Divide the cooked noodles into bowls and pour hot broth.

5. Top with desired toppings such as sliced green onions, tempura flakes, and nori seaweed.

6. Serve immediately and enjoy your homemade udon!

# SOMEN

## Ingredients:

- Somen noodles
- Soy sauce
- Mirin (sweet rice wine)
- Bonito flakes (optional)
- Green onions (optional)

## Instructions:

1. Cook some noodles according to package instructions.

2. Within a compact bowl, combine a mixture of soy sauce and mirin in a 1:1 ratio.

3. Drain cooked noodles and rinse with cold water.

4. Pour sauce over noodles and toss to coat.

5. Serve chilled, garnished with bonito flakes and green onions if desired.

# HIYAMUGI

## Ingredients:

- Hiyamugi noodles
- Broth (dashi)
- Soy sauce
- Mirin (sweet rice wine)
- Green onions, chopped
- Nori seaweed, sliced

## Instructions:

1. Cook the hiyamugi noodles according to package instructions and drain.

2. In a pot, heat the broth with soy sauce and mirin to taste.

3. Add the cooked noodles to the pot and simmer for a few minutes until heated through.

4. Serve the hiyamugi in bowls, garnished with chopped green onions and sliced nori seaweed.

5. Enjoy your delicious hiyamugi!

# NAGASHI SOMEN

## Ingredients:

- Somen noodles
- Ice cubes
- Cold water
- Dipping sauce (tsuyu)
- Toppings of your choice (green onions, ginger, shiso leaves)

## Instructions:

1. Set a pot of water to simmer and prepare noodles according to the package's instructions.

2. Rinse cooked noodles under cold water to cool them down.

3. Prepare a large container filled with ice cubes and cold water.

4. Place the container at one end of a long bamboo chute or plastic pipe.

5. Slide the cooled somen noodles through the chute or pipe into the icy water.

6. Catch the flowing noodles using chopsticks or a sieve as they pass by.

7. Serve the nagashi somen in bowls with dipping sauce and desired toppings.

8. Enjoy this refreshing summer dish by dipping the noodles in tsuyu and savoring each bite!

## Ingredients:

- 250g soba noodles
- 1 cup dashi broth
- 1/4 cup soy sauce
- Two tablespoons mirin
- One tablespoon sugar
- Wasabi, for serving
- Scallions, thinly sliced, for garnish

## Instructions:

1. Prepare the soba noodles per the directions on the package. Rinse and drain using cold water.

2. bring dashi broth, soy sauce, mirin, and sugar to a boil in a small saucepan. Let it cool.

3. Serve the chilled soba noodles on a bamboo mat or in a bowl. Dip each bite of soba in the sauce before eating.

4. Garnish with wasabi and scallions. Enjoy!

## KITSUNE UDON

## Ingredients:

- Two packs of udon noodles
- 4 cups of dashi broth
- One tablespoon of soy sauce
- One tablespoon of mirin
- One tablespoon of sugar

- Two pieces of aburaage (fried tofu)
- Green onions, sliced

## Instructions:

1. Prepare the udon noodles per the directions on the package and reserve.

2. In a pot, heat the dashi broth over medium heat.

3. Add soy sauce, mirin, and sugar to the pot and stir until dissolved.

4. Slice the aburaage into thin strips and add them to the pot.

5. Simmer for a few minutes until the flavors meld together.

6. Divide the cooked udon noodles into bowls.

7. Pour the hot broth with aburaage over the noodles.

8. Garnish with sliced green onions.

9. Serve hot and enjoy!

## YAKI UDON

## Ingredients:

- 200g udon noodles
- One tablespoon of vegetable oil
- Two cloves garlic, minced
- One small onion, sliced
- One carrot, julienned
- One bell pepper, sliced
- 150g shredded chicken or beef (optional)
- Two tablespoons of soy sauce
- Two tablespoons of oyster sauce
- Salt and pepper to taste

## Instructions:

1. Cook udon noodles according to package instructions, then drain and set aside.

3. Add the garlic and onion, and sauté them until they brown and

become aromatic.

4. Stir-fry the bell pepper and carrot for a few minutes or until the vegetables soften.

5. If using meat, add it now and cook until cooked through.

6. Add cooked udon noodles to the pan/wok, followed by soy sauce and oyster sauce. Mix well to combine all ingredients evenly.

7. To taste, add salt and pepper for seasoning.

8. Cook for another minute or two until everything is heated.

9. Serve hot, and enjoy your delicious yaki udon!

## TANUKI SOBA

## Ingredients:

- 4 ounces soba noodles
- One tablespoon of vegetable oil
- One small onion, thinly sliced
- Two cloves garlic, minced
- One carrot, julienned
- 8 ounces ground pork
- Three tablespoons soy sauce
- Two tablespoons mirin (Japanese sweet rice wine)
- One tablespoon sugar

## Instructions:

1. Prepare the soba noodles per the directions on the package. Empty and place aside.

2. Heat the vegetable oil in an enormous saucepan over a medium-high flame. Add onion, garlic, and carrot. Sauté for 2 minutes until softened.

3. Add ground pork to the skillet until browned and cooked through.

4. combine sugar, mirin, and soy sauce in a small bowl. Transfer the blend to the skillet containing the pork and veggies.

5. Stir well to combine all ingredients and let it simmer for about 5 minutes until the flavors meld together.

6. Serve hot cooked soba noodles. Enjoy your delicious Tanuki Soba!

## JAPCHAE (KOREAN-JAPANESE FUSION)

## Ingredients:

- 8 ounces sweet potato noodles (naengmyeon)
- Two tablespoons vegetable oil divided
- Four cloves garlic, minced
- One onion, thinly sliced
- One carrot, julienned
- One red bell pepper, thinly sliced
- 6 ounces spinach
- 4 ounces shiitake mushrooms, sliced
- Three tablespoons soy sauce
- Two tablespoons of sesame oil
- One tablespoon sugar

## Instructions:

1. Cook sweet potato noodles according to package instructions. Drain and set aside.

2. Melt a single tablespoon of oil made from vegetables in a big pan over medium heat. Add garlic and cook until fragrant.

3. Add onion, carrot, bell pepper, spinach, and mushrooms to the pan. Stir-fry until vegetables are tender.

4. mix soy sauce, sesame oil, and sugar in a small bowl. Scatter the vegetables with the sauce and toss to combine.

5. Include the cooked sweet potato noodles in the pan and thoroughly mix everything.

6. Cook for another minute or two to allow flavors to meld together.

7. Serve hot and enjoy your delicious Japchae!

# SUMPTUOUS SIDES

## AGEDASHI TOFU

### Ingredients:

- One block of firm tofu
- 1 cup of cornstarch
- Vegetable oil for frying
- 1 cup of dashi broth
- Two tablespoons of soy sauce
- Two tablespoons of mirin (Japanese sweet rice wine)
- Green onion and grated daikon radish for garnish

## Instructions:

1. To eliminate additional fluid, drain and maneuver the tofu.

2. Cut the tofu into bite-sized pieces and coat them with cornstarch.

3. In a deep pan or skillet, preheat the vegetable oil.

4. Fry the tofu until golden brown and crispy on all sides.

5. combine dashi broth, soy sauce, and mirin in a separate saucepan. Bring to a simmer.

6. Place the fried tofu in serving bowls and pour the hot broth.

7. Garnish with chopped green onions and grated daikon radish.

8. Serve immediately as an appetizer or side dish with steamed rice.

# GOLMAAL

## Ingredients:

- 1 cup spinach or other leafy greens
- Two tablespoons of soy sauce
- Two tablespoons sesame paste or tahini
- One tablespoon sugar
- One tablespoon toasted sesame seeds

## Instructions:

1. Blanch the spinach in boiling water for about 30 seconds, then rinse with cold water and drain.

2. mix the soy sauce, sesame paste, and sugar in a small bowl until well combined.

3. Add the blanched spinach to the bowl and toss until evenly coated.

4. Serve right away after adding a sprinkle of toasted sesame seeds. Enjoy!

# HIJIKI SEAWEED SALAD

## Ingredients:

- 1/2 cup dried hijiki seaweed
- One tablespoon of soy sauce
- One tablespoon of rice vinegar
- One teaspoon of sesame oil
- One teaspoon sugar
- 1/4 teaspoon salt
- Optional toppings: sesame seeds, sliced cucumber, shredded carrots

## Instructions:

1. Soak the dried hijiki seaweed in water for 10 minutes until it softens.

2. Drain and rinse the seaweed thoroughly.

3. mix soy sauce, rice vinegar, sesame oil, sugar, and salt in a bowl.

4. Add the rinsed hijiki seaweed into the bowl and toss well to coat with the dressing.

5. Let the salad marinate for at least 15 minutes to allow flavors to meld.

6. Serve as is or add optional toppings such as sesame seeds, sliced cucumber, or shredded carrots.

7. Enjoy your refreshing Hijiki Seaweed Salad!

# SUNOMONO

## Ingredients:

- One cucumber
- Two tablespoons of rice vinegar
- One tablespoon sugar
- 1/2 teaspoon salt

## Instructions:

1. Slice the cucumber thinly.

2. In a bowl, mix rice vinegar, sugar, and salt until dissolved.

3. Add sliced cucumber to the vinegar mixture and toss well.

4. marinate in the refrigerator for at least 30 minutes before serving. Enjoy!

# GOYA CHAMPURU

## Ingredients:

- One package of firm tofu
- 1/2 cup thinly sliced pork
- Two eggs
- One onion, sliced
- 1/2 cup bean sprouts
- 1/4 cup sliced carrots
- 1/4 cup sliced green bell peppers
- Two tablespoons of soy sauce
- One tablespoon of oyster sauce
- Salt and pepper to taste

## Instructions:

1. Drain and press tofu to remove excess water, then cut into bite-sized cubes.

2. In a skillet, cook the pork until browned. Remove from skillet and set aside.

3. In the same skillet, sauté onions until translucent. Add carrots and green bell peppers and cook for another minute.

4. Push vegetables to one side of the skillet and crack eggs into the space. Scramble until lightly cooked, then mix with the vegetables.

5. Fill the skillet with the tofu, pork, bean sprouts, oyster sauce, soy sauce, and season with salt and pepper. Stir well to combine all ingredients.

6. Cook for a few minutes until heated through and flavors are well blended.

7. Served hot with steamed rice as a main course or accompaniment.

Enjoy your Goya Champuru!

# KINPIRA GOBO

## Ingredients:

- Two large burdock roots
- One carrot
- One tablespoon of sesame oil
- Two tablespoons of soy sauce
- One tablespoon mirin (optional)
- One tablespoon sugar

## Instructions:

1. Peel and julienne the burdock roots and carrot.

2. In a pan, around a moderate flame, warm the sesame oil.

3. Add the burdock roots and carrot to the pan and sauté for 5 minutes.

4. mix soy sauce, mirin, and sugar in a small bowl until sugar dissolves.

5. Add the sauce to the skillet with the veggies and simmer for five minutes or until the vegetables are soft.

6. Serve hot over rice or as a side dish. Enjoy!

# NASU DENGAKU

## Ingredients:

- One medium-sized eggplant
- Two tablespoons of miso paste
- One tablespoon mirin
- One tablespoon of soy sauce
- One tablespoon sugar

## Instructions:

1. Set the oven's temperature to 400°F or 200°C.

2. Cut the eggplant in half lengthwise and score the flesh in a criss-cross pattern.

3. mix the miso paste, mirin, soy sauce, and sugar until well combined in a small bowl.

4. Brush the miso mixture generously onto the flesh of each eggplant half.

5. Arrange the cut-side eggplants on a baking sheet and bake until soft and caramelized, about 20 minutes.

6. Serve hot as an appetizer or side dish. Enjoy!

# JAPANESE PICKLES (TSUKEMONO)

## Ingredients:

- Two cucumbers
- One tablespoon salt
- Three tablespoons of rice vinegar
- One tablespoon sugar

## Instructions:

1. Slice the cucumbers into thin rounds or julienne strips.

2. Sprinkle salt over the cucumber slices and let them sit for 10 minutes to absorb excess moisture.

3. Rinse the cucumbers under cold water and squeeze out any remaining liquid.

4. In a bowl, stir sugar and rice vinegar until sugar is dissolved.

5. Add the cucumber slices to the vinegar mixture and toss well to coat evenly.

6. Let the pickles marinate in the refrigerator for at least 30 minutes, stirring occasionally.

7. Serve chilled as a refreshing side dish or condiment with your favorite Japanese dishes.

# LOTUS ROOT KINPIRA

## Ingredients:

- One lotus root
- One tablespoon of sesame oil

- One tablespoon of soy sauce
- One tablespoon mirin
- One teaspoon sugar
- Sesame seeds for garnish

## Instructions:

1. Peel and slice the lotus root into thin rounds.

2. Place the oil from the sesame seeds in a pan over medium heat.

3. Add the lotus root slices to the pan and stir-fry for 2 minutes.

4. mix soy sauce, mirin, and sugar in a small bowl.

5. Pour the sauce mixture over the lotus root and stir-fry for 3 minutes until tender.

6. Sprinkle with sesame seeds for garnish.

7. Serve hot as a topping for noodles or rice or as a side dish. Enjoy!

# CHILLED TOFU WITH TOPPINGS

## Ingredients:

- One block of firm tofu
- Two tablespoons of soy sauce
- One teaspoon of sesame oil
- Toppings (such as sliced green onions, grated ginger, crushed garlic, sesame seeds)

## Instructions:

1. Drain and rinse the tofu. Pat it dry with paper towels.

2. Cut the tofu into bite-sized cubes.

3. Combine sesame oil and soy sauce in a small bowl.

4. Drizzle the tofu with the soy sauce mixture and toss lightly to coat.

5. Place the tofu in the refrigerator to chill for at least 30 minutes.

6. Before serving, sprinkle desired toppings on top of chilled tofu.

7. Enjoy your refreshing chilled tofu with toppings!

# DELECTABLE DESSERTS
## MATCHA GREEN TEA ICE CREAM

## Ingredients:

- 2 cups heavy cream
- 1 cup whole milk
- 3/4 cup granulated sugar
- Two tablespoons of matcha green tea powder
- One teaspoon of vanilla extract

## Instructions:

1. combine the heavy cream and whole milk in a medium saucepan.

2. Over medium heat, raise the mixture's temperature to a simmer, being cautious not to let it boil.

3. whisk the granulated sugar and matcha green tea powder in a separate bowl.

4. Slowly pour the matcha mixture into the hot cream mixture, whisking constantly until well combined.

5. Switch off the heat source and mix in the vanilla essence.

6. Allow the mixture to cool completely, then refrigerate for at least 4 hours or overnight.

7. After the mixture has cooled, transfer it to a freezer-safe container and process it according to the directions provided by the manufacturer until it thickens.

8. Put the ice cream in a container with a lid and freeze it for at least 4 hours or until it solidifies.

9. Serve and enjoy!

# DORAYAKI

## Ingredients:

- 2 cups all-purpose flour
- 2/3 cup sugar
- Four large eggs
- One teaspoon of baking powder
- 1/2 cup red bean paste

## Instructions:

1. whisk flour, sugar, eggs, and baking powder in a bowl until well combined.

2. Lightly grease and heat a nonstick pan over medium heat.

3. Spoon batter into the pan in small circles and heat until bubbles appear on top.

4. After flipping, heat for a further minute or until golden brown.

5. Remove from heat and spread a spoonful of red bean paste onto one pancake.

6. Place another pancake on top to make a sandwich.

7. Repeat with the remaining batter and red bean paste.

8. Serve warm and enjoy!

# TAIYAKI

## Ingredients:

- 1 cup all-purpose flour
- Two tablespoons sugar
- One teaspoon of baking powder
- 1/4 teaspoon salt
- One egg
- 3/4 cup milk
- 1/2 teaspoon vanilla extract
- Red bean paste (or any desired filling)

## Instructions:

1. whisk out flour, sugar, baking powder, and salt in the bowl of a mixer.

2. Break the egg in a different bowl and mix in the milk and vanilla fundamental worth.

3. Whisk until a homogeneous batter develops, then gradually add the wet components to the dry ingredients.

4. Lightly coat a taiyaki pan with butter or oil and preheat it to medium heat.

5. Pour two tablespoons of batter into each mold and quickly place a spoonful of red bean paste in the center.

6. Cover the filling with another tablespoon of batter and close the pan tightly.

7. Cook, flipping halfway through, for about 3 minutes or until golden brown on both sides.

8. Remove from the pan and enjoy your warm teriyaki!

# JAPANESE CHEESECAKE

## Ingredients:

- 6 ounces cream cheese
- 1/4 cup unsalted butter
- 1/2 cup sugar
- 1/4 cup milk
- Three eggs
- 1/4 cup all-purpose flour
- Two tablespoons cornstarch
- One teaspoon of vanilla extract

## Instructions:

1. Set the oven's temperature to 325°F, or 165°C.

2. melt the cream cheese, butter, and sugar until smooth in a double boiler.

3. Remove from heat and whisk the milk, eggs, flour, cornstarch, and vanilla extract.

4. Pour the mixture into a lined baking pan.

5. Bake for about an hour until the top is golden brown and the cake is set.

6. Allow to cool completely before serving. Enjoy your Japanese cheesecake!

# ANMITSU

## Ingredients:

- One can of fruit cocktail
- 1 pack of agar agar jelly
- Three tablespoons of sugar
- 1 cup of water
- One scoop of vanilla ice cream

## Instructions:

1. Drain the fruit cocktail and set aside.

2. Dissolve the agar agar jelly and sugar in water over medium heat, stirring constantly.

3. Transfer the mixture to a square dish and allow it to solidify by cooling.

4. Cut the agar agar jelly into cubes.

5. Serve the fruit cocktail and agar agar jelly cubes in a bowl.

6. Top with a scoop of vanilla ice cream.

7. Enjoy your Anmitsu!

# DAIFUKU MOCHI

## Ingredients:

- 1 cup glutinous rice flour
- 1/4 cup sugar
- 3/4 cup water
- Red bean paste (optional)

- Potato starch or cornstarch for dusting

## Instructions:

1. combine the glutinous rice flour, sugar, and water in a microwave-safe bowl.

2. stir the mixture until it is fully blended and smooth.

3. Place a plastic wrap over the bowl and microwave it for two minutes on high.

4. Remove from the microwave and stir vigorously with a wet spoon.

5. Return to the microwave and cook for another minute.

6. Dust a clean surface with potato starch or cornstarch to prevent sticking.

7. Transfer the mochi dough onto the dusted surface and knead it until smooth and elastic.

8. Divide the dough into small equal portions.

9. Take one portion of dough and flatten it in your palm.

10. Place a small amount of red bean paste in the center of the flattened dough (optional).

11. Fold the edges of the dough over to enclose the filling, pinching them together to seal.

12. Shape into round balls and dust with more potato starch or cornstarch to prevent sticking.

13. Repeat steps 9-12 with remaining portions of dough.

14. Serve and enjoy!

# YOKAN

## Ingredients:

- 6 1/2 cups water
- 1 cup azuki beans
- 2 cups sugar
- One tablespoon agar agar powder

## Instructions:

1. Rinse the azuki beans and soak them in water overnight.

2. Drain the soaked beans and place them in a pot with water.

3. Once the saucepan reaches a boil, lower the heat and simmer the beans for around half an hour or until they become tender.

4. Add sugar to the pot and stir until dissolved.

5. In a separate bowl, dissolve agar agar powder in water, then add it to the pot.

6. Cook, stirring constantly, over low heat for approximately 10 minutes or until the mixture slightly thickens.

7. Turn off the heat and transfer the mixture into a plastic-wrapped square or rectangular mold.

8. Allow it to cool for approximately one hour at room temperature, then chill for at least three hours or until it solidifies.

9. Once set, remove from the mold, cut into desired shapes, and serve chilled as a traditional Japanese dessert called Yokan.

# KUZUMOCHI

## Ingredients:

- 1 cup kuzumochi powder
- 1 1/2 cups water
- 3/4 cup sugar
- Kinako (roasted soybean flour) for dusting

## Instructions:

1. In a saucepan, combine the kuzumochi powder and water.

2. Stir until the mixture is smooth.

3. Include the sugar and mix until it dissolves.

4. Transfer the mixture to the saucepan and simmer over a medium-high flame, stirring perpetually, until it hardens and turns translucent.

5. Pour the mixture into a square or rectangular dish and refrigerate for at least 2 hours or until set.

6. Cut the kuzumochi into bite-sized pieces and dust with kinako before serving. Enjoy!

# WARABIMOCHI

## Ingredients:

- 80g wasabi starch
- 400ml water
- 100g sugar
- Kinako powder (for dusting)

## Instructions:

1. Dissolve the warabi starch in water and set aside for 10 minutes.

2. heat the mixture over medium heat in a saucepan, stirring constantly until it thickens.

3. Add sugar and continue to stir until well combined.

4. Pour the mixture into a square dish and refrigerate for about 2 hours or until set.

5. Cut into bite-sized pieces and dust with kinako powder before serving. Enjoy!

# TAIYAKI ICE CREAM

## Ingredients:

- Taiyaki batter mix
- Ice cream of your choice

## Instructions:

1. Prepare the Taiyaki batter according to package instructions.

2. Heat a Taiyaki pan and lightly grease it.

3. Pour the batter into the molds, filling them halfway.

4. Place a small scoop of ice cream in the center of each mold.

5. Cover with more batter, filling up the molds completely.

6. Cook until both sides are golden brown.

7. Enjoy your delicious Taiyaki Ice Cream!

# HOMEMADE DASHI AND SAUCES

## AWASE DASHI

### Ingredients:

- 4 cups water
- One piece of kombu (dried kelp)
- 1 cup katsuobushi (bonito flakes)

### Instructions:

1. In a pot, add water and kombu.

2. Let it sit for 30 minutes to allow the kombu flavor to infuse.

3. Set the pot's temperature to medium and gently simmer it.

4. Remove the kombu from the pot Just before it reaches boiling point.

5. Add katsuobushi to the pot and let it simmer for another 5 minutes.

6. Strain the liquid through a fine sieve or cheesecloth to remove any remaining bonito flakes.

7. The resulting liquid is awase dashi, which can be used as a base for various Japanese dishes.

## KOMBU DASHI

### Ingredients:

- Two pieces of kombu seaweed (about 4 inches each)
- 4 cups of cold water

## Instructions:

1. Rinse the kombu seaweed under cold water to remove any impurities.

2. Place the rinsed seaweed and cold water in a pot.

3. Let it soak for at least 30 minutes or overnight in the refrigerator.

4. Set the pot on medium heat and cook it gradually.

5. remove the kombu seaweed from the pot before it reaches a boil.

6. Continue simmering the remaining liquid for about 10 minutes.

7. Remove from heat and strain through a fine-mesh sieve or cheesecloth.

8. The resulting liquid is your homemade Kombu Dashi, ready for use in various Japanese dishes!

## NIBOSHI DASHI

### Ingredients:

- 2 cups water
- 1 cup dried niboshi (small dried anchovies)
- One piece of kombu (dried kelp), about 2 inches in size

### Instructions:

1. To remove impurities, Rinse the dried niboshi and kombu under cold water.

2. combine the water, rinsed niboshi, and kombu in a saucepan.

3. Return the entire mixture to a boil over medium-high heat. After that, lower the heat to a simmer for five minutes.

4. Using a moderate flame, bring the mixture to a boil. After that, lower the heat to a simmer and let it cook for five minutes.

5. Strain the dashi into a bowl or container through a fine-mesh sieve or cheesecloth.

6. Niboshi dashi can be used in Japanese dishes like miso soup or noodle broth. Enjoy!

## HOMEMADE TERIYAKI SAUCE

### Ingredients:

- 1/2 cup soy sauce
- 1/4 cup water
- Two tablespoons brown sugar
- One tablespoon honey
- One clove of garlic, minced
- One teaspoon of grated ginger

### Instructions:

1. Mix all the ingredients in a small pot.

2. Once the sugar has dissolved, heat over medium heat while stirring continuously.

3. Simmer the sauce for five minutes, or until it has somewhat thickened, on low heat.

4. Before using, remove from heat and allow to cool.

5. Keep refrigerated for up to a week in an airtight container.

# PONZU SAUCE

## Ingredients:

- 1/2 cup soy sauce
- 1/4 cup rice vinegar
- One tablespoon of lemon juice
- One tablespoon of orange juice
- One teaspoon of sesame oil

## Instructions:

1. In a small container, combine the rind of the orange juice and lemon juice, rice vinegar, and soy sauce.

2. Stir in the sesame oil until well combined.

3. You can serve it immediately or keep it in the fridge for up to a week in a sealed container. Enjoy!

# TEMPURA DIPPING SAUCE

## Ingredients:

- Three tablespoons soy sauce
- Two tablespoons of rice vinegar
- One tablespoon mirin (sweet rice wine)
- One teaspoon sugar

## Instructions:

1. In a compact bowl, thoroughly combine the sugar, rice vinegar, mirin, & soy sauce.

2. Serve as a dipping sauce for tempura or other fried foods. Enjoy!

# GOMA DARE (SESAME SAUCE)

## Ingredients:

- 1/2 cup toasted sesame seeds
- Four tablespoons of soy sauce
- Two tablespoons of rice vinegar
- Two tablespoons mirin (Japanese sweet rice wine)
- One tablespoon sugar
- One clove of garlic, minced
- One teaspoon of grated ginger
- Water (as needed to adjust consistency)

## Instructions:

1. Toasted sesame seeds should be ground until a fine paste is in the bowl of a food processor or blender.

2. Fill the blender with the soy sauce, rice vinegar, mirin, sugar, ginger, and garlic. Blend until thoroughly mixed.

3. Gradually add water while blending to achieve desired consistency. Add more to make a thinner sauce; add less to make a thicker sauce.

4. Transfer the mixture to a bowl and let it sit for at least 10 minutes to allow flavors to meld together.

5. Stir before serving and use as a dipping sauce or dressing for salads, noodles, or other dishes. Enjoy!

# MENTSUYU (NOODLE SOUP BASE)

## Ingredients:

- 1 cup soy sauce
- 1 cup mirin (Japanese sweet rice wine)
- 1 cup sake (Japanese rice wine)
- 1/2 cup bonito flakes (dried fish flakes)
- 1/4 cup dried kombu seaweed
- Two tablespoons sugar

## Instructions:

1. combine soy sauce, mirin, sake, bonito flakes, kombu seaweed, and sugar in a small pot.

2. Cook for five minutes, simmering the mixture over medium heat.

3. Turn off the heat source and allow it to cool fully.

4. To eliminate particles, strain the mixture through a fine sieve.

5. Transfer the Mentsuyu noodle soup base to a bottle or jar for storage.

6. Use as a flavorful base for various Japanese noodle dishes or a dipping sauce for tempura.

# UNAGI SAUCE

## Ingredients:

- 1/2 cup soy sauce
- 1/4 cup mirin
- 1/4 cup sugar

## Instructions:

1. combine soy sauce, mirin, and sugar in a small saucepan.

2. Transfer the mixture to a medium heat source and stir until the sugar fully dissolves.

3. Cook the sauce for five minutes after a simmer.

4. Take it off the stove and allow it to cool before putting it in a bottle.

5. Drizzle the unagi sauce over your favorite dishes for added flavor. Enjoy!

## TONKATSU SAUCE

## Ingredients:

- 1/4 cup ketchup
- Two tablespoons Worcestershire sauce
- Two tablespoons of soy sauce
- One tablespoon honey
- One tablespoon of rice vinegar

## Instructions:

1. combine ketchup, Worcestershire sauce, soy sauce, honey, and rice vinegar in a small bowl.

2. Mix well until all ingredients are fully incorporated.

3. Serve straight away or store in the fridge for later use.

4. Enjoy with your favorite tonkatsu or other dishes!

# JAPANESE BEVERAGES

## GREEN TEA (MATCHA)

**Ingredients:**

- One teaspoon of matcha green tea powder
- 1 cup of hot water

**Instructions:**

1. Fill a cup with matcha green tea powder.

2. Add the hot water and whisk to dissolve and froth up the powder completely.

3. Enjoy your refreshing cup of green tea!

## SAKE

**Ingredients:**

- 2 cups of water
- One packet of sake yeast

**Instructions:**

1. Wash the rice in icy water until clear.

2. Use a rice cooker or the stovetop to cook the rinsed rice with two cups of water.

3. Let the cooked rice cool to room temperature.

4. Sprinkle the sake yeast over the cooled rice and mix well.

5. Transfer the mixture to a sterilized glass jar or container.

6. Use a cheesecloth or towel to enclose the jar and tighten it with a rubber band.

7. Store the jar in a dark, cool place for about 3-4 days, allowing fermentation to occur.

8. Once fermented, strain out any solids from the liquid using a fine-mesh sieve or cheesecloth.

9. Transfer the liquid back into clean containers and refrigerate before serving it.

# PLUM WINE (UMESHU)

## Ingredients:

- 2 pounds of Japanese plums (ume)
- 2 cups of rock sugar
- 4 cups of shochu (Japanese distilled liquor)

## Instructions:

1. Wash and dry the plums thoroughly.

2. make small holes in each plum for better infusion using a toothpick.

3. Place the plums and rock sugar in a sterilized glass jar or container.

4. Pour the shochu over the plums and seal the jar tightly.

5. Store in a cool, dark place for at least six months, shaking the jar gently every few weeks to mix the ingredients.

6. Once ready, strain the liquid into clean bottles and refrigerate before serving chilled. Enjoy.

# SHOCHU

## Ingredients:

- 2 cups sweet potatoes
- 1 cup rice koji
- 4 cups water

## Instructions:

1. Cut the sweet potatoes into little pieces after washing and peeling them.

2. Add water to the sweet potato cubes in a large pot. Bring to a boil and cook until the sweet potatoes are very soft.

3. Mash the cooked sweet potatoes using a potato masher or blender until smooth.

4. Allow the mashed sweet potatoes to cool to room temperature.

5. Mix well with rice koji to the cooled mashed sweet potatoes.

6. Transfer the mixture into a clean glass jar and cover with a cheesecloth or plastic wrap.

7. For approximately a week, keep the jar in a cold, dark place and stir once daily.

8. To remove any particles, separate the blend through cloths or a filter with a fine mesh after a week.

9. Transfer the liquid into clean bottles and seal tightly.

10. Leave the bottles in a cool place for at least two weeks for fermentation to occur before enjoying your homemade shochu.

**Note:** This recipe makes Koji-Shochu by fermenting sweet potatoes with rice koji. Traditional shochu production involves distillation, but this recipe provides instructions only for fermentation without distillation for an alcohol content of approximately 10-15%.

# YUZU CITRUS DRINK

## Ingredients:

- Yuzu juice
- Honey
- Sparkling water
- Ice cubes

## Instructions:

1. In a glass, mix yuzu juice and honey to taste.

2. Add ice cubes.

3. Top off with sparkling water.

4. Stir gently and enjoy your refreshing yuzu citrus drink!

# RAMUNE SODA

## Ingredients:

- One bottle of Ramune syrup
- One bottle of sparkling water
- Ice cubes

## Instructions:

1. Fill a glass with ice cubes.

2. Pour the Ramune syrup into the glass, filling it about 1/4.

3. Pour sparkling water into the glass gradually until it is nearly complete.

4. Gently stir the mixture to combine the syrup and sparkling water.

5. Serve immediately and enjoy your refreshing Ramune soda!

# CALPICO

## Ingredients:
- 1 cup plain yogurt
- 1/4 cup sugar
- 1/4 cup water
- 1/2 teaspoon vanilla extract

## Instructions:
1. combine the yogurt, sugar, water, and vanilla extract in a blender.

2. Blend until smooth and creamy.

3. Transfer the blend into a bottle or glass.

4. An hour or more before serving, place in the refrigerator.

5. Serve chilled, and enjoy your homemade Calpico!

# AMAZAKE

## Ingredients:
- 1 cup cooked rice
- 3 cups water

- 1/4 cup koji rice

## Instructions:

1. In a blender, combine the cooked rice and water.

2. Blend until smooth and pour the mixture into a pot.

3. Add the koji rice to the pot and mix well.

4. Cover the pot with a lid and let it sit at room temperature for around 8-10 hours or overnight.

5. After fermenting the mixture, strain it through cheesecloth or a fine-mesh screen to eliminate any solids.

6. Transfer the liquid to a clean container and refrigerate until chilled.

7. Serve cold as a refreshing drink or use it as a sweetener in various recipes. Enjoy!

# SUNTORY HIGHBALL

## Ingredients:

- Ice cubes
- 2 oz whisky (preferably Suntory Toki)
- 6 oz soda water
- Lemon peel or wedge (for garnish)

## Instructions:

1. Add ice chunks to a prepared highball glass.

2. Pour the whisky over the ice.

3. Top up with soda water.

4. Stir gently to combine.

5. Garnish with lemon peel or wedge.

6. Enjoy your refreshing Suntory Highball!

# THE END

Printed in Great Britain
by Amazon

54185744R00062